LIBERTY
DANCEHOUSE

A SMALL BUT POWERFUL
BOOK ON PERSONALITY AND PURPOSE

KEHINDE FAWUMI

Illustrations by Dare Adetuberu

Inner layout design courtesy AquaPub

Cover Design by Jaydee Cassidy for AquaPub

LIBERTY
DANCEHOUSE

A SMALL BUT POWERFUL
BOOK ON PERSONALITY AND PURPOSE

KEHINDE FAWUMI

To my translator – Olayinka
To my family, for their love
To God, for this inspiration

"The greatest tragedy of life is not death but life
without a purpose - life with the wrong priorities.
Life's greatest challenge is in knowing what to do.
The greatest mistake in life is to be busy but not
effective. Life's greatest failure is to be successful in
the wrong assignment."
- Dr. Myles Munroe

"Liberty Dancehouse" is a metaphor for a place of
liberty from the fears, limitations and worries of our
lives. It is a location in our life's journey where we
find purpose and are driven to take calculated actions
towards achieving the purpose. It is a state of
fulfilment - being successful in your purpose,
or achievement of a major goal in our lives.

I have written this book to walk with you on your
path to your Liberty Dancehouse.

CONTENTS

SECTION ONE

Liberty Dancehouse

CHAPTER ONE
Broken Roads

Chapter One
Broken Roads

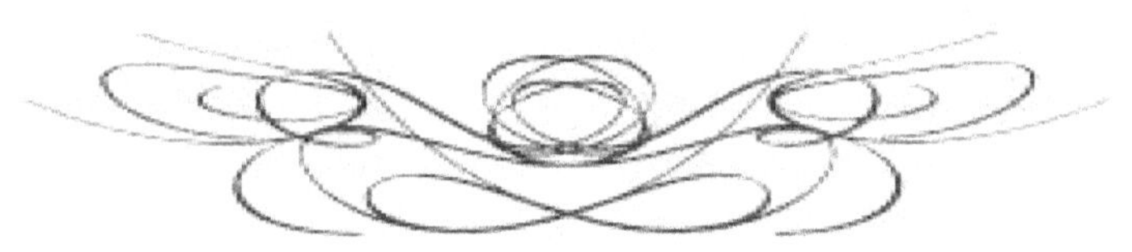

"This doesn't seem right!" Ela finally grumbled with a frown.

"Are we really walking down this long broken road? What if we can't find a Dancehouse anywhere around?" She questioned fearfully.

"It is dangerous to walk around in the night. There could be dangerous people at the corners. Or even wild animals. We could get lost and not be able to find our way back. It is safer to stay home!" Ela complained.

Poor Ela is being persuaded by her best friend and roommate, Agna, to take a decision against her best interest.

Naive Agna would not welcome any thought that could jeopardize her chance of finding good music in a Dancehouse! Her mind was made up. "I need some music! I will not be happy if I remain here." she reiterated, convincing Ela for the umpteenth time, who quite helplessly had to agree.

"This way!" Agna led while Ela followed reluctantly.

Agna and Ela are college students in their early twenties. One could think of them as sisters, not only because of their closeness,

but also because of the striking resemblance in their looks. People had often taken one for the other.

Their personalities however, are quite unalike. Agna is an extrovert and likes to force her opinions on others. Ela on the other hand, is a calm listener and slow to speak. While Agna jumps to conclusion on matters quickly and easily; Ela internalizes them, thinks over and again, considers possible alternative meanings and then comes up with well thought-through conclusions.

In effect, boredom means different things to them. To Agna, boredom is the lack of activities. To Ela, boredom is the lack of internal drive. Agna is bored when there is nothing to do, Ela gets bored when there is no passion to do a thing.

Agna feels lonely when there is no one around, Ela feels alone instead. To Ela, "aloneness" and "loneliness" mean different things. Aloneness, to Ela, is a positive feeling of the need to stay out of the noise of everything external in a bid to listen to oneself.

So, while Agna sulks over the absence of friends, Ela remains calm and activates her creative self. "Not hearing the noise of others around, helps you hear yourself" Ela would argue. Agna, of course always disagreed. "It is no fun to be alone! It sucks!" she claimed.

Ela is able to differentiate the noise of her ego from the voice of her intuition. Thus, she could focus on observing little things and effect changes wherever needed. She had trained her mind to develop insights and new ways of looking at things. By listening to herself, Ela learnt to remain positive about everything around

her - good or bad.

Agna often challenges Ela's philosophies about emotions and negative feelings. One peculiar scenario was a day Agna failed in an exam and felt sorrowful about it. Ela gave a homily that fell on her friend's deaf ears.

"Anytime challenges and situations arise to lock you in a negative emotional state, the most important thing to do is to change the way you perceive the situation! You can always consider what other meanings the situation could have, and then change your interpretation of the situation by choosing the meaning that most empowers your mind. When you learn to remain positive in any situation, it becomes easy to come out of the frequent states of sadness, loneliness, inadequacy, and hurt" Ela advised.

Agna did not succumb. She argued that emotions are not easily changed by some philosophical put downs.

Also, music means different things to them. To Agna, music is only a solution, a remedy to an undesirable feeling of loneliness. To Ela however, music means much more. Music to her is the rhythm that brings her deep joy and a strong sense of purpose. Music revives her passion for her dream and aspirations. Music helps revive her positive energy and strength.

Agna and Ela are very passionate about music. Their passion could easily be mistaken for an addiction. Music will easily top the pyramid of Agna and Ela's hierarchy of needs. It is at the core of their needs.

"We all need some music in our lives, and we must find ours!" Agna remarked with a questionable confidence, spotting an abandoned building in the

middle of a field sideways to the lonely road on which they walked.

"Without music, life can be frustrating." She continued, hoping to win her friend's interest.

"I have a funny feeling about this." Ela simply replied, gathering some motivation. "Let's see where this will lead us." She tied her scarf and caught up with her friend.

One could picture the scenery. They walked on dilapidated roads in

a remote neighbourhood at sunset. The mild breeze caressed their tender skins but also tortured their feet with a mix of dried leaves and dust. There were a few old buildings standing by the road. One couldn't tell the color of the paintings on the buildings as they've had their turns of the atmospheric chemistry. Agna and Ela argued about the possibility of the buildings being habitable for humans.

As they lolloped along the road, they began to feel strange as there were practically no other person on the road. After a while, they noticed that the path was becoming narrower and soon ended! It was a close.

"I knew this would happen. You take decisions too rashly." Ela murmured.

Agna stood there, disappointed and uncertain about what to do. She wore an uncharacteristic mien as her excitement eroded away. Her confidence about finding a Dancehouse is now weakened. She clearly would not want to go back home but there seem to be no way forward.

"You might just be right, Ela. We may not find a Dancehouse anywhere around." Agna said finally, looking towards Ela for motivation.

"Well, we already set out on this mission and we must get to the end of it. We should not give up so easily." Ela said, choosing to stay positive. "Let us try the other direction. At least, then we stand a chance of finding a Dancehouse. If we stop now, then we absolutely have no chance."

It was a long and boring walk back on the same road they already explored. They cheered themselves as they walked back, noticing buildings, signposts and warning signs they didn't pay attention to at first. "I'm beginning to see the benefit of walking a road twice. You discover things you normally wouldn't discover!" Agna said, stating the obvious.

"Sometimes life lessons are repeated until learned. Lessons are presented to us in various forms until we have learned them. Learning does not end. There is no part of life that does not contain its lessons. If you are alive, there are lessons to be learned." Ela explained.

Ela and Agna are getting to interpret their uncomfortable situation as an opportunity to learn lessons. Their courage to take on a new path in finding a Dancehouse shows their readiness to take risks. Reaching the Dancehouse, for them, is a goal that must be achieved however slim the chance may look. They understand that they don't have to figure it all out to start, but they have to start to figure it all out. They are willing to do at present, what others won't do, in order to have in the future, what others won't have.

Ela stopped to think for a while and wrote on the floor "You'll get lost, but don't stay lost."

Sadly, the new path did not turn out as the answer they sought. It led them to a junction where they had to choose between three possible routes. Worse still, there were no clear signs that any of these paths would lead to a Dancehouse.

They had three options: a) gamble and follow a path blindly, b) listen and follow their guts and c) give up!

Clouded by their predicament, they gambled and sauntered into a random road. "This must lead somewhere!" Agna encouraged.

By now their paces were slower and shorter. They got discouraged and lost the desire to push hard. It was uncertain where the road would lead. Since they gambled, there was a chance it was the wrong choice.

It became hard to read road signs and to pay attention to their environment. Nothing else mattered to them than to see where the road would lead. The walk became monotonous. Agna would regret if their efforts again come to futility.

They apparently did not expect it would get so tiring and uninteresting. Since they were already half-way down the road, it was undesirable to go back. They made a few bends in the direction they deemed fit but still no indication...no hope of reaching a Dancehouse.

"I have seen this building before. We've been here!" Agna grumbled. They've been moving in circles. "How come we did not realize this earlier?" She lamented. "We don't deserve this! Why should it be so difficult to find music and dance?" She exclaimed sadly.

"Perhaps broken roads are part of the grander plan" Ela said in a bid to console her friend who is now angry and disappointed. "There may be important lessons to learn from our plight. Sometimes it's good to fail, it helps us get the proper perspective on success" Ela's words did not impress Agna in the least.

"When we set out on another path, if we do, we will be sensitive to our movement as we may be going in the wrong direction, running in circles or even going backwards." Ela again chose to see the situation from a different perspective.

Although tired and unmotivated, they knew they have a choice to make. They could either continue the search for a Dancehouse or give up. Considering the unpalatable experiences they have had, coupled with the lingering uncertainties of finding a Dancehouse, the choice to continue the search is unappealing.

If the poor girls will find a Dancehouse, they will need to let go of the unpleasant experience of their rat race, embrace their present circumstance and imagine the possibility of still finding music. If they choose to take a decision based on their past experiences, they are certain to miss the future. But the quicker they can let go of the past, the sooner they are able to embrace the present and imagine the future.

"I'm out of here! I go no further." Agna submitted. She had weighed their options and concluded there was no chance of success. "It is safer to return home. That's our comfort zone. That's what we know!" She shuffled to a nearby tree and stood still.

Ela was confused. She knew Agna was right in many ways, but her guts seemed to be telling her differently. Somehow, she believed there is still a chance that they attain their goal. "There may be a Dancehouse around the corner…" She mumbled.

"Don't be so foolish Ela." Agna said with a well-meaning attitude. "It's darker now and cold. And there is no Dancehouse anywhere close."

Ela knew it would be impossible to convince Agna otherwise. So instead of saying anything, she started walking slowly in a new direction, hoping Agna will change her mind and follow. If she does, then Ela will have to guarantee that the road leads to a Dancehouse…and the road had better lead to one.

CHAPTER TWO

Northern Stars

Chapter Two
Northern Stars

It's difficult to describe the emotion Agna felt.

It's a mix of frustration, sadness and anger. She was totally unprepared for the endless unproductive expedition. She wanted to turn back and leave, but she thought she would be betraying her friend.

"It was my idea to find a Dancehouse in the first place." She soliloquized, dropping her head. She was definitely unhappy about their unanticipated situation and was starting to lose her excitement for being at the Dancehouse.

"The longer you stay on the wrong road, the quicker you lose your passion for success." She mumbled as she watched Ela pace gently ahead of her. Agna was fast losing her drive for her goal and would need to regain her passion in order to stay focused and motivated.

Ela heard Agna's mumblings but decided to keep quiet. She ruminated about the ease of feeling frustrated when walking on the wrong paths. About how we easily get dragged down, unmotivated and sometimes agonized when doing things that are not meant for us.

"It's frustrating to walk on wrong roads" Agna whined again.

Ela, quiet still, walked on slowly hoping to find possible indications of a nearby Dancehouse. She is again *alone*. As her culture was, she started thinking about the possible reasons for being in their unforeseen mess.

"Could it be because we did not plan purposefully, or ask important questions before setting out on the road?" She thought. "Perhaps because we were too impatient in taking the decision about where to go."

Ela considered many possible causes of their misadventure. She considered the possibility of having made a hasty decision. "Agna coerced me into this" she complained, realizing the need for her to stand by her decisions and follow her heart rather than live to impress others. She reflected on these important lessons.

Then she wondered if she had taken the right decision to continue the pursuit of finding a Dancehouse. It didn't seem so, judging from the prevailing facts. Many thoughts flooded her mind – mostly negative. She again feared the possibility of not finding any Dancehouse the whole night.

She began to strengthen her mind by dwelling on thoughts that would empower and motivate her to keep moving forward. "What if the long broken roads are actually leading us to the Dancehouse?" She

mused with a sigh. "What if the broken roads and the misfortunes are the northern stars giving us directions to the right road?" She thought aloud. Agna had been shuffling along. She still wondered if anything good would come out of their expedition. However, she had been listening to Ela speak to herself. Ela's last words caught her attention and she sneered "You are simply unreasonable! Can't you see this is getting us nowhere?"

Ela had not done anything to deserve Agna's condescending comments. However, Ela would not be discouraged by these words, rather she chose to revive her excitement and belief in the chance for success. "Sometimes you have to be unreasonable to be able to follow your heart" She replied.

After few more minutes of walking on a road that seemed endless, something remarkable happened. Just when it seemed all hope was lost, then it happened, standing right ahead of them, a signpost that reads "Liberty Dancehouse!" It was illegible, since they tried to read from afar.

It was Agna that sighted it first. The letters from the half-rust signpost looked blurry. It is obvious that it had not been cleaned in a while. The mixture of dust and water had precipitated dirt which made it difficult to read from it. Only the picture of a half-aged man with a musical instrument gave her a sense of hope that something good may be close.

She advanced in the direction of the signpost, her heart racing faster. She could not think of anything else but to finally find a clear direction on the sign post. She said a little prayer in her heart.

As she moved closer, apprehensive, she began to notice what would be the most joyful news she had received. Right in front of her was a signpost which reads: **Liberty Dancehouse:** *Liberated to liberate others!*

It is tougher now to describe the emotion Agna felt. It is a mix of excitement, awe and gratitude. On the verge of giving up, when it seemed their journey was hopeless, they felt a stirring of hope. They've been right at the edge of breaking through but couldn't notice it. And they would have given up if the sign post had not showed up.

"It is better not to try at all, than to try and give up in the end!" Ela said with a mild smile, gratitude was written all over her.

They looked ahead and saw the Dancehouse, beautifully decorated and glowing in the dark! The soft music oozing out from afar melted whatever negative emotions remaining in them. "Wow, it is a cool Dancehouse!" Agna exclaimed. "Let's go dance away boredom!"

Ela was calm for a moment as she again mused over some key takeaways from the *miracle* that just happened. "We should in fact be thankful for the broken roads which led us straight to the Dancehouse" She emphasized. "It was a rough experience, but well worth it."

Although they could see their destination in a short distance,

Agna and Ela have one last hurdle to confront.

There seem to be no direct link to the Dancehouse from their position. There are dilapidated paths which lead to other destinations but not to the Dancehouse. Thus, to reach the Dancehouse, they will need to walk back and follow a new path.

This time, it was easy to decide to walk back and follow a new path. They are happy to take the walk. The knowledge of their destination has energized them to face any hurdle that may delay their arrival, it drove away any doubt or discouragement that could arise. They realized clearly that the mental disturbances they've had, had been because of their uncertainty about their destination. When they had no clear mental picture of the location of the Dancehouse, they worried

about everything and even expected that things would go wrong. Their reason for the expedition was challenged as long as they couldn't define their destination.

"Finding out one's 'Why' changes everything about one's journey." Ela said with a sigh. She now had a better understanding of the reasons for her past failures. "My past failures were simply because I had no definition of my 'Why'" she thought.

Agna could not argue this. She's had her past mistakes and failures due to her inability to define her purpose.

"Ela, you know I once got the chance to audition for a big music show but I blew it because my passion was too weak to fight for it." Agna started. "I spent more time nurturing my addictions to drugs and alcohol rather than prepare adequately for the audition. I was totally unmotivated. The judge told me that I had a great potential, but I needed to show them that I cared

L
Liberty

more about my career than my addictions." She said soberly. "I didn't even show up for the final audition because I was angry and discouraged, so I quit. I lost a great opportunity."

"It's easy to lose when you do not define the reason for fighting", Ela interrupted.

"Still not a week goes by that I do not regret it! I have learnt never to quit. It'll hurt, but I'll outlive the pain because when it hurts, then it counts!" Agna concluded.

Ela was touched by her friend's story, but she has hers to tell. "Until two years ago, I never understood my real purpose for living. Everything I did was only by gamble. I basically did what everyone asked me. I joined many groups that I was not supposed to. I did many irrelevant things because I had no idea what I wanted." Agna nodded as Ela spoke regrettably.

"I dated the wrong guys because I had no clear understanding of the kind of relationships I wanted. All the relationships ended bitterly for me. I took the wrong jobs and followed wrong friends simply because I did not understand my purpose. Then I started to feel worthless and frustrated. I believed I was not good enough in anything I did, so I always expected to fail when I tried to do things, and I basically failed in most things. I just believed everyone else was better than me." Ela sighed.

"Then I met someone who told me some words I'll never forget. He said: "Everyone is a genius, but if you judge a fish by its ability to climb a tree, it will live its whole life believing that it is stupid." He made me realize that finding my 'genius' will revive my self-esteem and confidence and in turn, make me feel better about everything around me. And that was what happened."

"Welcome to discovery!" They hugged and cheered themselves.

They were now close to the

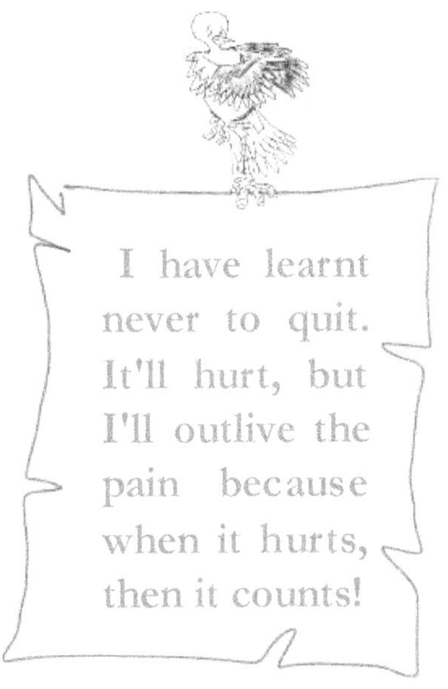

Dancehouse. The music was louder and the excitement was rising. "The feeling of getting to your destination is magical" Agna said. "This is it! This is what we have toiled for. We are closer to it now. I can feel it. It'll be the most exciting night of my life!"

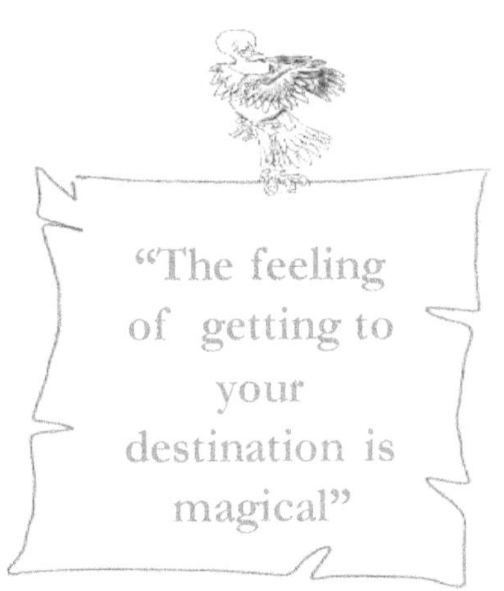

Agna heard a familiar music and was already dancing to the tune of it. Her shawl dangled on her neck as she moved her head to the rhythm of the music, left to right like an oscillating simple pendulum. "This is my type of music!" Agna exclaimed with a bright smile. She felt her boredom and discomfort evaporate in the face of the music.

She envisioned herself in the Dancehouse. She pictured the sight of the Dancehouse in her imagination: the DJ to the left and the bar to the right. Seven groups of couples in the middle of the floor dancing in synchronization to the bass buzz of the soft music. The music being played was a mixture of Blues and Jazz.

It was a female musician singing. Her beautiful soprano voice switched flawlessly from major to minor keys as the rhythm permitted. Her voice was enough to calm any storm in the soul.

There were also a few teenage ladies on the floor, ready to mingle. They sang along with the music, hitting high notes with strong passion and love, grateful for that moment.

Everything was clear in Agna's imagination. She was there in the Dancehouse in her mind, though her body was a few hundred meters away. She felt a deep sense of elation and wished she was already in the Dancehouse. The imagination of her desired destination had beautified her mind. Even though she was not there yet, everything in her could already experience the bliss of music.

Imaginations are powerful, they paint pictures in our minds; more real than reality, more certain than certainty. They help us see things not as they are but as they might be. They give us a taste of what we should feel at best and a peep into what we could become.

"The joy of achieving one's goals is superior to the pain of discouragement!" Agna muttered.

Ela had been internalizing some thoughts and she was starting to soliloquize again. She would get excited about an important thought and just hum some words. Her paces became shorter and slower. She felt ecstatic and peaceful. It was a magical moment for her.

It was as though some higher invisible being was speaking words to her. She could hear it clearly in her mind even though there were no sounds. She was totally immersed in the moment, unaware of her environment. She stayed silent and listened to that voice speaking inside her.

"Sometimes life gets us against the ropes and hits us hard. Many people give up when they get hit and they never get up. Many people miss their way and never retrace their steps. Many people fall down and never rise up to persist. It is not how strong you start that matters but how well you end. Many people start their journeys with strong motivation but give up on the way. Some people never even start at all because they feared that they will never be able to finish." Ela nodded as she listened to the voice.

"It is helpful, sometimes, to confront difficult situations at certain points in life. Some obstacles in people's lives are hindrances from the real distractions of life. They help them look inwards for courage to focus on the things that matter", continued the voice.

"Therefore, overcoming obstacles is one tool required in the work shed of people aspiring to be successful. Success can be measured by the magnitude of the obstacles overcome to achieve it. Sometimes when tough situations come into people's lives, they are there to lead them to the right destination. They are fine messes. They are only bends, not ends!"

Ela was lost in her thoughts as she walked along with Agna, moving closer to the Dancehouse. Unawares, she started humming her thoughts: "It's usually the fear of the uncertain that holds us back from plunging ourselves into our endless possibilities." Ela said, speaking to herself. "We can't connect the dots looking forward; we can only connect them looking backwards. So, we have to trust that the dots will somehow connect in the future. Believing that the dots will connect down the road gives us the confidence to follow our hearts - even if it leads to the well-worn path." She sighed with a nod.

Then she remembered some inspiring words she had read earlier that night. On an article in an old newspaper were written the inspiring words: "We cannot always control our environment, but we can always control our attitudes. How we respond to circumstances is determined by our attitudes. The circumstance itself should not control our attitude; else we become manipulated by the environment. We should always endeavour to respond positively with self-control and optimism."

"Yes!!!" She screamed, throwing her fist in the air. She had realized the reasons many people fail to live the life they had imagined.

She threw herself up in excitement and said in a loud voice, "There are no mistakes, only lessons!" She had learnt something that would change her reasoning.

As they took their last few steps to the Dancehouse, Agna and Ela wiped their faces and tidied themselves. Agna adjusted her dangling shawl, sprayed her expensive perfume and fixed her dress.

They could not wait to share the lessons they had learnt from their seeming predicament. They now have a second purpose for going to the Dancehouse. They would be custodians of some important lessons for the new friends they would meet at the Dancehouse. They definitely did not expect to learn a great deal from such an unexpected situation. Somehow, they trusted the process and got the best out of it.

"Here we go!" Agna said, taking that memorable step into the Dancehouse.

CHAPTER THREE
Writings on
the Wall

Chapter Three
Writings on the Wall

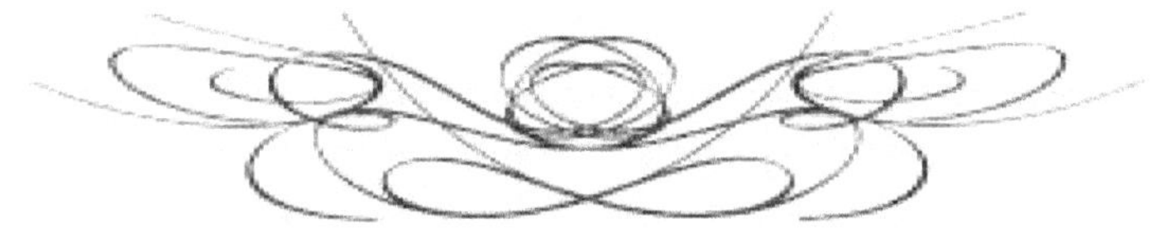

One thing that attracts anyone to Liberty Dancehouse is the beautiful exterior and interior decorations. The building is adorned with the right blend of pure paintings amplified by green background shades. The interior is also impressively furnished to the taste of the visitors. The dance floor is illuminated with colorful lights and drawings vivid enough to entice the most boring dancer.

Agna and Ela undoubtedly loved everything about it. Their imaginations couldn't have captured the ecstatic mood in the air. Although there were people of different kinds, everyone exhibited a deep sense of bliss.

As Agna sauntered into the Dancehouse, she went directly to the bar. "A glass of water please." She asked with a forced politeness. A gentle young man attended to her with a confident look. "You must be new here." He asked with a bright smile. "Oh yes!" replied Agna, forcing a smile. "Welcome to Liberty!" He complimented, handing her a glass of water.

Ela marvelled at Agna's extroverted act. She wondered how easy it was for her to mingle so quickly. She looked around, observing every detail of the dancehouse. She was impressed by the pomp and joy in the air. Then she heard a man shout from afar: "Dancing makes you happy, makes you feel free!" Everyone cheered and made a toast: "Only cowards won't dance! Toast to bravery!" They laughed and moved about as the DJ turned up the music.

Everyone comes to Liberty Dancehouse to find their own inner peace and comfort through music. The Dancehouse represents a safe and serene place for them to forget the pains of their past and confidently take actions in the line of their true purpose. People who visit Liberty are driven by three main factors. Most people visit because they have hurt enough that they need to find comfort. Others visit because they have learned enough that they want to find inner peace and dance. Few others visit because they have enough resources that they are able to reach the Dancehouse. Essentially, different reasons draw people to the Dancehouse.

No matter the troubles and challenges that had haunted the people, they regarded Liberty as a turning point for themselves. To them, music is the passion they need to activate their aspirations, dreams, purposes, positive energy, creative thinking and desires. Music drives away every form of negative emotions and energizes them to get back their strength and move towards greatness.

In effect, everyone looked forward to the music and to showcase their own unique dances. Dancing means different things to different people at Liberty. To some, dancing connotes

their resolute determination to take calculated steps in the direction of purpose. To others, dancing is navigating to the place of happiness and comfort. Generally, dances are usually expressions of people's decisions to make lasting changes in their lives, to welcome a new era of their lives and to make happen what they had always wanted.

It's a proud thing to dance at Liberty Dancehouse! Dance is everyone's aim.

It is customary that anyone who visits Liberty write down their favourite impressions based on their Liberty-experience. At the Dancehouse, there are impressions written on the walls by past dancers as a memorial for themselves and for other visitors. These impressions are written in deep reflection of their plights and their moments of truth.

Agna looked up and found perhaps the most inspiring impression written by an orphan who was dying of cancer. Story had it that she lost her parents in a ghastly accident when she was five. Yvette, who should only enjoy peace, suffered from chronic lymphocytic leukemia. Initially, the Doctor told her that the disease had only affected her bone marrow and blood, that there may be a chance for her to be treated. However, after two weeks, she got the worst news: her disease had spread to other important organs including her spleen, liver, and lymph nodes. So when the Doctor told her she only had one week to live, she knew she had to find the Dancehouse, albeit late, to experience the sweetest bliss she could find before *going to rest*.

In her last few hours at Liberty, she wrote those words with tears, her hands shaking vigorously: "There is something worse than death; it is lack of music and inability to dance courageously."

There was another touching story of young Lady Bee who was molested at her early age by her own uncle. Poor Lady Bee

had to live with her unmarried uncle because her parents could not afford to finance her education. The cruel uncle took advantage of her and destroyed her innocence, leaving her in deep agony for the rest of her life.

Lady Bee lived with the stigma for years. She hated every man that came her way and felt unworthy to live a joyful life.

Her hurt drove her to Liberty - where she found joy again. As she danced to the music, those words came to her: "Dancing helps you forget your despair, helps you build an edifice of hope from the broken pieces of your past."

Lady Bee realized it was her own mind that kept her in bondage. It was the self-inflicted anger, anguish, unforgiveness and negative attitudes which dominated

her mind, that limited her. As she danced, she suppressed her past feelings and decided to change her perception. She made up her mind to keep making positive choices in her life. She found joy again.

One of the most popular impressions on the wall was written by Mr. Ade. Before he located Liberty, he had lost all his savings and investments and was bankrupt. His worst nightmare couldn't have prepared him for this unforeseen predicament. He soon began borrowing and

begging for help from people whom he trusted. Everyone disappointed him. He wallowed in that gloom for ten years, depressed and dejected. He lost every inner motivation he had left. He was obscured and couldn't see a good life for himself and his family.

The night he found Liberty, he was going to commit suicide. As he walked into the woods, making sure no one would easily find his rotten corpse, he heard rhythms of music that initially angered him but later calmed his nerves. One step at a time, he moved towards the Dancehouse. As he entered the hall, he experienced the kind of peace he had sought for ten years. Then he danced.

Before he left, he wrote these remarkable words: "Don't give up, don't ever give up. Stay Happy. Forget your dance-less situation, embrace the present, dance to the music." Then he began to reflect on how foolish he was to ever consider taking his own life. He wondered what would have become of his family if he wouldn't be there for them. As he thought, he wrote another impression: "Not everyone will get the chance to dance: some will not reach the Dancehouse, some will be discouraged by their challenges."

By now Ela and Agna had shifted their focus from the activities around them. They were more drawn to the inspiration in the air.

As they danced, a man walked up to the wall and wrote some words he had been thinking about for a while: "Fulfilment does not come by chance, it comes by dance!" He looked at it and nodded with a huge smile. He got it! The words he's

been meaning to express for some time. Then he quickly added another: "Don't be afraid to dance! Dancing is a choice, you can stay bored even when there's music."

Inspired by this man, Ela shunned all shyness and walked up to write her own first impression. It was borne out of a reflection on the unpredicted experience that led her to the Dancehouse. Ela smiled as she walked up the wall, she confidently wrote words that would inspire lots of future dancers: "Your will to dance must supercede the pains of your plight."

She looked around and read other impressions on the wall. She saw one which inspired her so much. It read: "Trust your dance, it may be out of beat but not out of purpose". As she read different inspiring writings from different kinds of people who wrote under the influence of music, she thought out loud: "We may hear the same music, but they mean different things to us." She decided to write it down.

Agna was lost in her euphoria. The music and

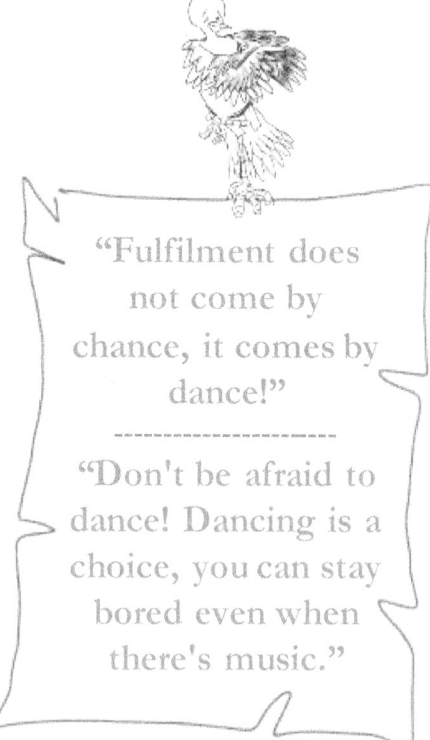

excitement in the Dancehouse had brightened her. What she had longed for had finally come to her. She found good music – the remedy to her undesirable feeling of loneliness. She gave less attention to Ela; music and dance were all she wanted after all.

She was very impressed by everything around her, especially the dances by elated people who were otherwise dejected and hopeless. Agna thought: "Observing others dance inspires you to dance." She looked at every corner of the hall and was inspired by it all.

She became thankful for the broken roads that led her to the Dancehouse. She thought to herself: "What if we had given up and turned back? What if we did not take the risk of stepping out in belief that we would find the Dancehouse? What if we had yielded to our fears?" She shrugged and made a nice turn as she danced. The DJ had played one of her favourite song and she sang along loudly:

It's not enough to hear the music.
Just Dance!
It doesn't matter if it's out of beat.
Just dance
Forget your annoyance and dance!
Find your balance and dance!

...

Agna was lost in the delight of the song. She closed her eyes gently and sang aloud so beautifully, hitting every note with perfection! As she sang, she began to imagine herself singing at the biggest music show in the world. In her mind, she had over a million people in the audience listening passionately to her.

For a moment, she remembered the opportunities she had lost in the past and felt the pain. But as she sang, she felt a deep sense of joy. At that moment, she resolved to have another bite at the cherry and give herself a second chance with the music audition she abandoned in the past.

Unknown to her, dancers at Liberty had gathered around, listening to her sing. They were all mesmerized by her awesomeness. As she opened her eyes, she could not believe what she saw. Everyone stood in front of her cheering with a heartfelt gratitude. She quickly made a turn and completed the song with a bow.

"Cheers to courage!" A man announced. "Cheers!" responded everyone.

Ela had a huge smile on her face as the dancers returned to their positions. She is, for the first time, deeply impressed by Agna's extroverted act.

CHAPTER FOUR

Sound of
Silence

Chapter Four
Sound of Silence

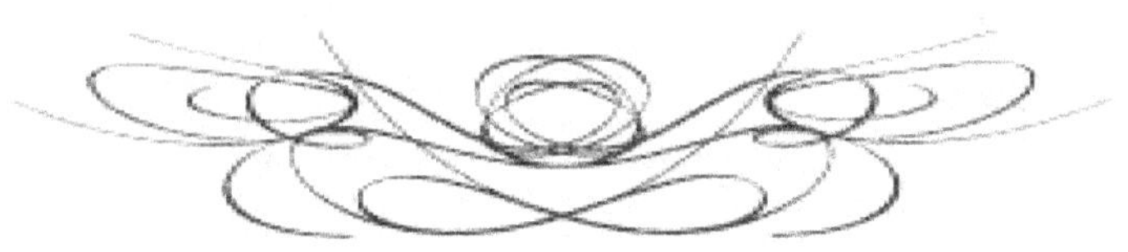

Ela sighted some people gathering around an impression written in big bold letters few meters away from the DJ.

Three men and two ladies standing with seemingly surprised looks as they gazed at the words written on the wall. They seemed to be inspired and excited about what they had discovered. Ela became curious. As she moved closer, she saw the inspiring words, written in inconsistent penmanship: "To dance is to be out of yourself. Larger, more beautiful, more powerful." She nodded in agreement, lifted up her glass and made a toast to the new inspiration.

Adjacent to the wall was a young lady who stood unmoved by the pageantry at the Dancehouse. She seemed lifeless. Not one of her limbs moved. On her partly torn clothes were blood stains which she attempted to cover meticulously. Her feet shot out of her wet shoes - which she wore wrongly.

For many minutes she stood in one position observing everyone express their inner joy. The look on her face reflected a combination of confusion and despair. She stood numb and watched others enjoy the bliss of Liberty.

Ela had noticed her earlier but ignored her. But as she made a new toast, she observed her again, unmoved. The lady made no sound, no movement and no smile.

Ela marvelled at the unexpected circumstance and decided to approach her. As Ela moved closer, the lady bent down as if to write something on the floor. But then she crawled to a side and burst into tears. Then Ela became more concerned.

"Could it be that she had not been able to overcome her misery? Perhaps her feeling of regret cuts very deep that she had lost hope for any possible change" Ela pondered. "Excuse me, is everything okay?" Ela questioned in a low gentle voice. The lady turned towards her but made no sound. "Do you need anything?" Ela persisted. "I am Ela, and you are...?" Ela stretched her hand in a bid to shake hers. Then she cracked up. A mixture of tears and mucus fluid ran down her delicate face but she didn't care.

"Everything will be fine, you are here now. That's all that matters!" Ela consoled. Still the lady did not say a word. She cried on. "Just listen to the music, you will find your peace." Ela continued. "Everyone here came with a deep hurt, but they chose to focus on the music rather than wallow in their pains."

The words from Ela were consoling and beautiful. The problem however was that the lady could not hear them. She is deaf.

46

Somehow, Ela could not imagine the possibility of having a deaf at Liberty. The ability to hear and correctly interpret sounds are supposedly prerequisite to finding joy and dancing at the Dancehouse. In her assumption, it is unexpected for the deaf to be at Liberty.

The lady gathered the little courage remaining in her and signed the words: "I am Louis. And I am deaf."

Ela stood startled. But she signed back quickly: "Nice to meet you Louis. Sadness and regrets belong outside of here. You are here now, that is all that matters!"

"I have lived with pain and regrets all my life! I am always a misfit and an embarrassment to whoever seem to show me friendship." She signed, making sure to keep low, the sounds which came out as screams as she expressed her despair.

Louis is perhaps the most unpopular person at the Dancehouse. She is easily unnoticed as she never interacted with anyone. She doesn't bother to speak because she felt her voice would sound awkward since she can't hear it. Her pathetic story is one she has never been able to tell anyone, partly because she is not proud of it.

She never knew, never knew how she became deaf. The only thing the doctor told her was that she suffers from a hereditary deafness.

Her mother divorced her father as soon as she realised Louis was deaf. She left the baby alone with the father, blaming him for the deafness of the poor toddler. She claimed that Louis' father possessed the dominant gene which was responsible for Louis' hearing loss.

She ranted as she walked away, raining insults and curses on her own husband. "I will not allow my life to be ruined like yours and your hopeless daughter" she cursed, packing the final pieces of her belongings. Louis' father stood shocked and said nothing.

The helpless man couldn't take care of Louis. He soon withdrew from any responsibility on her, stating that it is not worth investing in a child who will never be able to hear or speak a word. So he ostracized Louis for some months and later sent her off to a school for the deaf.

Louis' father took to his heels once he handed the baby to the school. He had given wrong and unreachable contact details and addresses. Louis never had contact with any of her family again. So, she never knew, never knew how she became deaf.

Louis grew up to the realization that she would never be able to hear any sound, or enjoy TV, or listen to the radio. Her deafness would not allow her enjoy the bliss of music. She would never be able to know the sound of animals. She often wondered if she would ever be able to find someone who would love her, or get a job, or have friends who would truly care for her. For many years, she felt intense grief and would have committed suicide if she had not been stopped and rescued.

She had felt grief, shock and denial, countless times. "I cannot be deaf!", she would whine. "This can't be me!"

Finding friends was difficult for Louis. Since she was grieved with the pain of denial from her family, she did not understand love. The hatred she felt for her parents was massive. She also experienced betrayal from men who only dated her for sex. They all used her and left her disappointed. The last man she dated gave the same excuse like others: "It would be a disgrace to me and my family if I married a deaf girl!"

Then she swore never to give in to any man again.

Louis would give anything to become like others. She would do anything to be able to hear sounds. She tried a couple of tricks but none worked. Then she got angry at the realization that there was nothing she could do...that she is deaf!

Two weeks before Louis crawled into Liberty, she had the most shameful experience of her life. A random man, Mr. Tutu, who knew Louis' parents way back, travelled for business and encountered Louis' mother in a distant city, twenty years after she left her family. The woman was shocked to meet Mr. Tutu. She stuttered as she greeted him. Their conversation was short-lived as they both were unprepared for the near-shameful meeting.

Mr. Tutu came back and disclosed the news to Louis.

Louis gathered all her savings, despising her hatred and travelled twelve hours painfully trying to locate the woman whom they told her was her mother. The journey itself was hell. It was hard for her to ask direction since she was deaf.

When she finally reached the location, it was late in the night. She approached her mother, who was now married to another well-to-do man with three beautiful girls.

In her rags, Louis introduced herself to the woman hoping she would take her in. The woman denied her and chased her away, threatening to jail her if she ever came to her again.

That night, her disability completely won over her courage and she felt an unbearable pain. She ran as fast as she could aiming to drown herself in a nearby river. She screamed as she ran, her worst nightmare had taken over her. She was overwhelmed with darkness and a pain that would never leave her life. She didn't cry, what she felt was beyond tears, so she simply screamed her guts out.

She dove right into the river and prayed her death came sooner. She intentionally opened up her mouth so she could drown faster. Lying there in the river, closer to death than ever before, she closed her eyes and said her last words.

One would have thought she was dead if she had not opened her eyes to find herself laid beside the river. She had been rescued, yet another time, by onlookers who saw her when she dove. Two young men stood beside her asking all kinds of questions. She heard nothing, only lips moving chaotically.

She stood up, disappointed, walked as fast as she could into the bush, no aim where to go. She kept walking, hoping some wild animal would bounce on her and tear her apart. She imagined and prayed that the worst would happen to her.

It was while she walked, in deep regret, that she noticed Liberty afar off. "A building in the middle of nowhere?" She questioned. "What could possibly be in the building?" She thought. Then she remembered a fable she had learnt from her literature teacher.

The fable had the story of a priest who killed wanderers and used them to appease his gods. The priest once captured a King while hunting and attempted to offer him as sacrifice to his gods. However, the sacrifice was rejected by the gods because the king was disabled.

Lots of thoughts rushed through her mind, all pointing to possibility of a close danger. She did not fear however, she was tired of living and would run into any danger even if it meant being sacrificed to a nameless god.

Undaunted, she walked towards the building, curious to find out what could possibly be inside. Unlike every other person who located Liberty, she could not hear those calming sounds of music oozing out of the building. However, she had some form of curiosity which made her, for the short moment, forget her desire to die. She began to imagine herself inside the building.

Louis was not prepared for what she saw inside the building. As she finally stepped into Liberty, she saw people of all colors and ages, dancing and supposedly-shouting to some music which she could not hear. Witnessing all that brought back memories of her inability to hear. She again felt bad for her sad life. She stood still, making sure no one noticed her, and simply watched.

After a while, she saw a man who rushed to a wall as though he is being chased by a thought, he wrote: "Listen to the music, dancing is only a product of listening." It was then she bent to the floor in a bid to write: "Does the deaf deserve to be happy?" But she couldn't. She simply crawled to a side and burst into tears.

Looking up, she saw someone standing in front of her with a

concerned smile and a stretched hand as if to shake her. Then she cracked up. A mixture of tears and mucus fluid ran down her delicate face but she didn't care.

She realized that the lady in front of her seemed to care a lot, but had no idea she was deaf. Then she gathered the little courage remaining in her and signed the words: "I am Louis. And I am deaf."

Ela decided to help Louis get out of her gloom and find joy again. She told Louis perhaps the most important words she ever heard.

"We are all deaf in one way or the other" Ela started. "We all have our weaknesses: physical, mental or spiritual. Our ability to focus on our strengths rather than our weaknesses is what matters."

"But why me? Why am I different from others?" Louis signed, interrupting. "Why do you have to be like others? Being different makes you unique and special." Ela emphasized.

"But I am deaf, I can never experience the joy of music. I can never find my dance. Deafness is my disability, it limits my life." Louis complained. She was filled with despair as she thought of her inability to experience inner peace. Deafness to her is her disadvantage, obstacle, adversity, lack, deficiency and unforeseen contingency. It was her excuse for her inability to find fulfilment.

"You should see things

differently. Being deaf is a blessing, not a curse. It helps you focus on what really matters." Ela made a strong impression on Louis with those words. "Being deaf isn't all that bad. It means you wouldn't have to listen to the shit music others listen to." She continued with a chuckle. "It is in deafness that you hear yourself, shunning all the distractions around you to reach deep to the deepest part of your creativity."

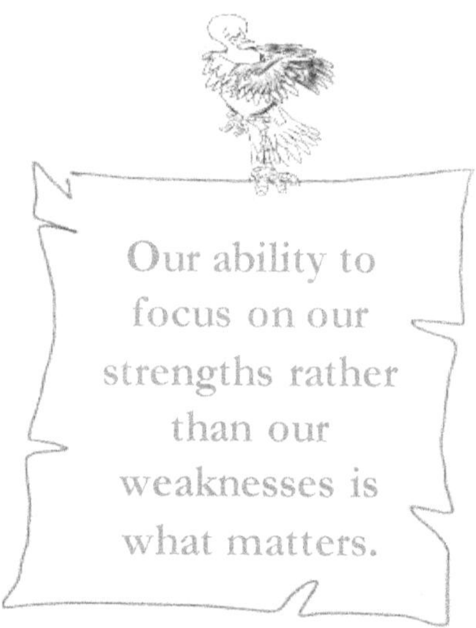

Louis focused on Ela's face as she signed those great words that drove deep into her soul. Every word from Ela made a strong impression on Louis. As Ela spoke on, Louis began to lose the consciousness of the lights that shone brightly on her face. She thought less of the people around her. As though in a trance, every other thing seemed to disappear one after the other leaving only Ela in front of her. She released her folded arms and relaxed her neck. She could feel her own pulse in her wrists. Nothing else was there with her other than Ela.

Being deaf isn't
all that bad. It
means you
wouldn't have to
listen to the shit
music others
listen to.

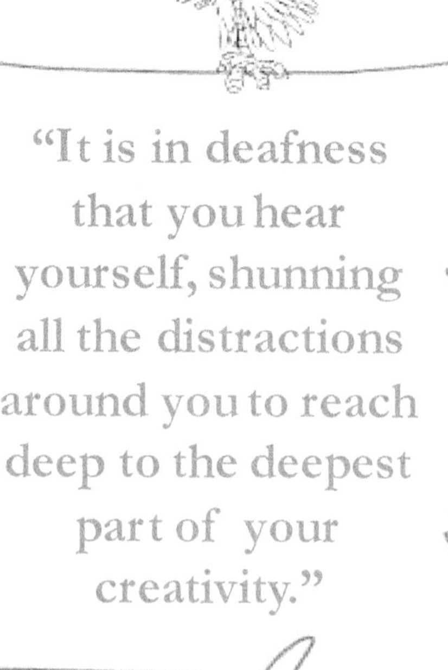

"It is in deafness
that you hear
yourself, shunning
all the distractions
around you to reach
deep to the deepest
part of your
creativity."

"Sometimes if you're different, then you need a different music." Ela signed calmly, touching her softly on her left arm as though to hypnotize Louis. Then she continued: "Not hearing the music helps you create yours. It's real music when it comes from within you. Creating your own music helps you forget your deafness, it gives you full control over the lyrics. So, be your own musician, groove to your own music. Hear the music in your soul, it's more meaningful."

Then Ela began to sign the words of the song being played in the room. Louis was drawn to every word signed by Ela. She lifted her hands, spread them to her sides as if to fly, and landed them on her thighs. Their movements were synchronized. When Ela raised her head, Louis simply did the same. She smiled as Ela signed the song making Louis reach deep down to find courage to dance.

Then Louis began to forget the pains of her past. She had been able to overcome her fears and was starting to find inner peace. At that moment, her disability did not bother her, she felt her heartbeats and imagined herself living and enjoying the same pleasures as anyone else. She felt her inabilities disappear in the face of courage and will to dance.

Louis closed her eyes. She imagined herself in a world where everything was perfect for her. In that world, she had lovely parents who loved her very much. She was living with her parents in a mansion beautifully decorated. She could hear and speak fluently in ten different languages. She had her dream job and had everything she wanted. She had no fears, no disappointments and no hatred.

Lost in her imagination, Louis began to move to some rhythm only she understood. She's found her own music! She began moving to the unheard melody of the song, as though she could actually hear the sounds. Louis enjoyed the delight of her new experience, basking in the bliss of her dance.

For several minutes, Louis danced to her own music. With some help from Ela, she found her own way to do what felt impossible.

By now, Louis was ready to write the strongest impression she had gotten from this experience. She opened her eyes, walked up to a wall and wrote as boldly as she could: "Everyone needs a translator. A friend who hears what you cannot hear."

She stepped back, read her own notion and smiled. Then she wrote again: "Don't ignore the signs of your translator, they tell the meaning of the music." And underneath it: "Sometimes, trusting your translator is the only way to understand the music."

Ela felt fulfilled as she signed the music with great pleasure. She, too, had learnt a great lesson from this experience. She wrote

down a few thoughts that came up on her mind: "Success is not always about hearing the music, but making yours. So, create your own music!"

As she thought about Louis again, she wrote: "No matter how deaf you are, you can still dance. "

As Ela wrote on, a few people gathered to read and learn from her inspirations. For every notion she wrote, someone made a toast. "Translate the music, share the experience. It's more fun! Helping others achieve their dreams helps you achieve yours" Everyone understood she was talking about living a life of impact. Helping others find their own purpose and brightening them with one's own light.

Ela felt a sense of fulfilment in a way she had never felt before. She seemed to have found her own rhythm. She discovered that, helping others find their own music gives her the truest sense of fulfilment. "This feels right!" She said with a smile.

Louis stood close and read as well. Something came to her mind and she gently wrote as people watched: "If the music is boring, change it or turn deaf!" Everyone sighed at this writing, they were all deeply touched by the

profoundness of the words. Louis spilled out those words aiming to communicate an important lesson she had learnt.

She had come to understand that her deafness was actually not the reason she was not dancing, it was her ignorance, pessimism and lack of motivation to shun her deafness, discover her own rhythm, create her own music and dance. Her ability to dance and being deaf are two different things.

"We really don't hear with our physical ears, hearing is first of the soul." Louis thought. She removed her tattered shoes, flung them in the air and danced on.

SECTION TWO

Liberty Dancehouse

CHAPTER FIVE

The Liberty Experience

Chapter Five
The Liberty Experience

Life's greatest challenge is knowing what to do - being able to clearly define one's purpose. Our journey in life is simpler once we have a defined purpose for living. Living through life becomes simpler, not complicated. Thus, the key to simplifying life is clarity of purpose. With a clear purpose, we are able to prioritize the important and relevant things in our lives. It is frustrating to live life fulfilling the wrong assignment.

The feeling of living life with a clear purpose is liberating and ecstatic. True sense of fulfilment, inner peace and freedom comes when we finally discover what we are carved out for. A life with a clear purpose is a fulfilled life.

In our pursuits in life, we all journey towards our liberties; we seek true freedom from fears and worries. Everyone's journey is different, but essentially, we all seek similar destinations. We are all driven by some dreams, visions, aspirations, passions, desires...by some music. The more interesting your music is, the more motivated you are to actualize it. It is our music that draws us towards our purpose, and keeps us going in the face of challenges.

Nothing splendid has ever been achieved except by those who dared to believe that something inside of them was superior to their circumstances. Every achiever has always understood the necessity of having an innate desire and passion, strong enough to keep them unwavering in the face of difficulties in the pursuit of their goals.

However, most of us are afraid to follow our passion because of the fears we nurture in our lives. We magnify our seeming inabilities, disadvantages, obstacles, lacks, deficiencies, negative situations and adversities; and blame our inactions on them.

In order to attain our desires, we must maintain a strong passion and positivity about our lives. We have all it takes to become whatever we wish ourselves to be.

In the following paragraphs, I described some principles that are important in the journey of living purposefully and experiencing liberty. You will learn that whatsoever you desire of good is yours. Only stretch your hand and possess it. Start out now, grasp the positive and be positive.

If you are not comfortable with your present lifestyle, then take actions to change it. You are responsible for what you are presently and your actions and decisions today will ultimately determine what you will become tomorrow. So spend quality time to discover yourself. What actually your hobbies are, your philosophy of life and passions. If you don't know what you want, every dung will be meal.

Take actions in line of your purpose. Dance. If needed, change your patterns and challenge your norms, shun negative habits, embrace happiness. You can always make happen what you've always wanted by the actions you take today.

Heroes have a rough time because they stand up when they ought not to, they speak when they ought not to; they always have to go that extra mile to attain their dreams. They dance. - *George Foreman.*

Fulfilment does not come by chance, it comes by dance!

Walk the Broken Road

"There is a Dancehouse around the corner..."

Launching into the unknown is an endeavour most of us are hesitant to undertake. Understandably because of the uncertainties involved and the risk of getting lost. The readiness to plunge ourselves into the pool of uncertainties is however important to reaching our goals. Every courageous step we take in resolute faith brings us closer to the realization of our dreams.

I thought about Ela and Agna walking in the midst of uncertainties, no idea whether a Dancehouse is *one mile away or fifty miles away*. However, they were keen on taking the chance, albeit slim, to find music and dance. Whether or not they would find a Dancehouse is a question no one could answer at the onset. There is of course a high chance they would not. But the strong feeling in their innermost being that they would achieve what they set out to do opened the way for possibilities. The expectation that something good would happen energized their goal and gave it momentum. When the impossible has been eliminated, whatever remains, no matter how improbable, is possible.

The 2016 UEFA European Football Competition took the world by shock. No one would have expected that the Portuguese National team would win the competition. Most bets were on the giant teams like France, Italy, Spain, Germany and the likes. However, at Euro 2016, Portugal won its first ever major trophy, defeating the host France 1–0 after 120 minutes play time.

Portugal was, on all grounds, one of the least expected teams to win the championship. All odds were against them.

Firstly, the national team had never won any major trophy in their football history. They had failed severally. The team reached the semi-finals of Euro 2000 but were defeated by the French team. They also lost at the semi-finals of 2006 World Cup and Euro 2012. They hosted the Euro 2004 competition and played

Greece in the finals. Unfortunately, they lost painfully 1 to 0. They seemed incomplete in football with very few medals to their name in history.

It was hard for a team who had lost severally at very important games to play confidently at the finals of the Euro 2016, especially when playing with the strongest team and host of the tournament, France. Portugal was clearly the weaker side in that final match.

Secondly, the journey of the Portuguese team to the Euro 2016 finals was a rough one. They finished 3rd in the group stage and only qualified because the tournament was *unwisely* expanded to 24 teams. More so, they did not win any game within the 90 minutes of the play time throughout the tournament.

One positive thing about the team however was that they had Cristiano Ronaldo, a striker who, at the moment, is arguably the best player in the world. He was seemingly their only hope for winning. Unfortunately, Cristiano Ronaldo was forced out of the final match by a knee injury just after 23 minutes, leaving only the unpopular players on the pitch.

Whatever chance Portugal initially had was now wrecked!

Strange enough, the Portuguese team did not waver in their drive to win. Even when every odd was against them, they kept playing with a positive spirit. They kept walking the broken road. And to the shock of the world, they went on to defeat the French team by a goal scored by Éder at the 109th minute.

Anything is possible when we allow ourselves to explore our possibilities. The fear of failure is worse than failure itself. When we fail to confront our fears, we deprive ourselves the chance of ever winning. As long as we choose convenience over conviction, we excuse ourselves from reaching our greatest potentials.

Fortune is evasive and can only be sustained by purpose and courageous actions. Whatsoever you desire of good is yours. Stretch your hand and possess it! Don't be afraid to walk the broken roads. If you have skills apply them! The world and you will profit from them. You need no permission from anyone to perform.

Fortune waits upon every wise step you take with courage. Grasp the positive and be positive.

There was the story of a young man, who once drove up a cliff and had an accident. He crashed into a pile of abandoned objects lying on the tip of the cliff. He had not paid close attention to the pile. He was however saved by a shrub to which he held firmly while he cried for help. "Is anyone there to help?". He heard a voice speak back to him: "I will help if you can trust me, release yourself from the shrub. I will catch you before you crash into the abyss".

Considering the reality that he's a dead man if he released himself from the shrub, he felt disappointed and shouted: "Is there anyone *else* there to help?"

How many times have we asked such questions? "Is there an *easier* way to go?" "Is there anyone *else* there to help?"

The most painful thing is that we never get an opportunity to live a full life as long as we yield to our fears and consider mediocrity over excellence. Jack Canfield says: "Don't worry about failure. Worry about the chances you miss when you don't even try."

We all are sometimes faced with unfair and undeserving situations which weigh us down. The worst decision anyone could take is to accept defeat! Any time hurting situations appear in our realities, we must learn to reach deep down our hearts and find courage to keep moving forward. We must seek strength in our weakest times and happiness in the saddest moments. "The heights by great men reached and kept were not attained by sudden flight, but they, while their companions slept, were toiling upward in the night." - Henry Wadsworth Longfellow.

The fear of failure is all in our minds. It is our mind that keeps us in bondage and holds us back from striving for what we desire deep within. However, like Ela, we can learn to change the way we perceive every situation. We have the greatest influence on our own thinking, imaginations and interpretations.

We can't always control our environment, but we can always control our attitudes. It's how we react to situations, not the situations themselves that influences our chances for success or failure. One important thing is to be able, at any moment, to sacrifice what we are feeling for what we should feel at best; what we are for what we could become.

No matter how broken, inconvenient or rough, walk that road!

Thank the Broken Road

"Sometimes, broken roads are northern stars giving us directions to our destination"

It is hard to be grateful for a painful experience.

No one would naturally be thankful for a heartbreak or for losing a job or failing in an exam or losing someone dear to one's heart.

It is natural and important to acknowledge that a painful experience has occurred and to feel the pain of it. It is normal to feel disappointed, sad and grieved when going through a difficult situation.

However, what we discover over time is that, in many situations the so-called unfortunate situation was necessary for a major breakthrough in our lives. But, since it is impossible to see the future at the time of the difficulty, it is difficult to understand how the challenge would lead to a bigger breakthrough.

Thus, the point of being grateful for a seemingly negative occurrence is about dealing with the negative emotions we feel. It is about trusting in faith that everything will make sense in the end. That the broken roads are part of a grander plan.

In order to be able to truly overcome our pains and challenges, we should learn to be grateful for the circumstances of our lives. It is in gratitude that we truly conquer our pains. What most people do however is to wallow in the negative emotions and remain stagnant, unable to move forward with their lives.

Every feeling we have, good or bad, is not based on the actual reality of life. Rather, our feelings are based on our interpretations of what things mean. Most situations that weigh us down are not bad in themselves, and we can always identify a joyful message in the midst of the situation.

Once we learn to perceive a situation in a positive manner, we can change how we ultimately feel about the situation. Then it becomes easy to trust that somehow, the difficulty is a blessing in disguise.

I once heard the story of an African king who had a childhood friend. That friend had a very positive view on all things around them; he was a constant optimist. No matter what happened in life, he always said the same thing: "This is good!"

The King and his friend hunted games together for many years. They were very skilled and devised good strategies for their hunting. The friend would prepare and load the weapon for the king, and the king will shoot the weapon. Thus, they were able to hunt down the cruelest and most dangerous animals.

One day, the king and his best friend went hunting, and on that hunting trip his friend misjudged. He fumbled with the rifle, and a bullet accidentally escaped from the weapon. The gun exploded and took off one of the king's thumbs with it. A bitter scream pierced the forest, the king screamed in great agony! His friend had mistakenly shot him, damaging his thumb forever.

The friend, seeing this, exclaimed: "This is good!"

"How can this be good?" Fumed the king. "This is NOT good!"

Upon their return, the King ordered the friend thrown into the deepest prison.

Months passed, and the king's injury slowly healed. His hand was getting stronger, and his desire to go hunting finally made him plan a most extravagant trip to a far-off land. This time he went alone.

As he moved close to his destination, he was caught by a group of vicious cannibals, who took him to their village to use as sacrifice to their gods and prepare a feast from his flesh.

But when they saw that his thumb was missing, they sent him on his way, because it is bad luck to eat an *unwhole* person in their culture. The king was over joyous, his friend's "blunder" had saved his life.

Upon his return, he immediately had his friend freed, and as the friend stepped out of his cell, blinking at the light, the king said: "I am sorry my dear friend, you were right all along, it was good that I lost my thumb. It was wrong of me to put you in jail." "No, no!" Laughed the friend. "It was good! Your majesty, if I wasn't in jail, I would have been with you, and the cannibals would have eaten me."

Gratitude is about strengthening the thoughts and meanings that brighten our daily lives and help us maintain a positive attitude in the midst of challenges. Someone once said: you are not sad because things are bad, rather things are bad because you are sad. Our lives are not judged so much by what happens to us as by the attitude we display in the face of what happens.

At some point in my life I was going through a heartbreak. I had made futuristic plans based on the relationship and everything seemed well and in place. So, when the unexpected happened, I felt a strong pain deep within me. I knew I had to choose between wallowing in the feelings of regrets and disappointment or to embrace a different meaning to the occurrence.

It could be that I needed to be out of the relationship in order to allow someone else into my life. It could be that now that I am out of the relationship, I can focus on the other important things in my life. Sometimes, we need to break out of relationships because of the negative influences they have on our lives.

There are endless positive reasons why an unexpected event, any unexpected event, could be a blessing in disguise in our lives!

It became easy for me to be freed from the pains caused by the heartbreak once I began to consider and strengthen the alternative, equally powerful and positive meanings of the break up.

While I admit that it is natural to feel hurt and pain when going through hard times, I also think that every negative situation comes with a positive message that we must identify. We must never limit our creativities by thinking in a unidirectional manner, when we can explore other possibilities and consider the interpretations that empower us.

A man who won a national title once said: "I want to thank all my obstacles, failures and adversities for making this possible!"
Be thankful for the broken road.

Envision the Dancehouse

"Finding out one's WHY changes everything about one's journey."

To be able to reach our goals and attain our dreams in life, it is important to hold a strong mental picture of our aspirations.

Thankfully, man has the great gift of imagination. Our mind is able to imagine the greatest things of life. We are able to see hundreds years into the future and imagine what our lives could be like. All limitations disappear in the realm of our imagination.

Thus, we can create clear mental pictures of our goals in our minds through imagination and by consistently holding on to positive thoughts about our possibilities. Any picture real in our imagination will ultimately attract its material equivalence and appear in our realities as we take the right actions towards it. As a man continues to think in his heart, so he becomes.

When we hold on to the mental picture of our destination, we are drawn closer to it and eventually, the picture in our imagination becomes our reality. In effect, there are actually no limits to our possibilities. At any moment, we have more opportunities than we can act upon.

"When we imagine our dreams, our vision expands. Expecting something to happen energizes us to take actions and gives us momentum. We often find that life responds to our outlook. What we expect to happen happens. The dreams we choose to believe in come true." - Anonymous

The only limitation to the manifestation of our vision is therefore the level of awakening it receives from us.

I cannot overemphasize the importance of fixing our focus on our intended destinations. If we do not know where we are going, we will not know how to get there. Having a clear mental picture of our destination is the key to reaching it. We can make happen anything in our lives once we have a clear vision and deliberately take steps in the direction of that vision.

Our present circumstances have been shaped by the steps we have taken in the past; and our future will be shaped by the actions and decisions we make today. Thus, we must learn to imagine everything we want our future to be like. We must visualize a better future and explore our endless possibilities, first in our imagination. By visualizing our goals, we can get our subconscious to work towards making these mental pictures come true.

Our imagination influences our thinking. By imagining a better and greater future, we will in turn naturally think of things not as they are but as they might be. We will see things from the perspective we have created in our minds. And since our actions are fueled by our thoughts, we are more energized to take actions and attract the resources and support we need to facilitate the attainment of our dreams.

Embrace the Big Picture

"...there indeed exist Liberty, a reality that is bigger and better than they had imagined..."

Attaining the greatness we imagine for ourselves will require radical self-development and growth.

Truth is, if our present personalities and capacities are enough to bring us to our destinations, we will already be there, or close enough. We must realize the need for deliberate continuous development of our minds and ultimately our lives.

In this journey, we must maintain a positive mental attitude and see the big picture. Since the future we imagine is bigger and better than the present, we must strive to work hard on ourselves, accept new mindsets and philosophies and take responsibility for our lives. The path to our destination will require us to embrace new realities and see beyond our stereotypes and prejudices.

The ability to see the big picture helps us become flexible and ready to change. It helps us understand that there exists other realities, different from ours, that when embraced could help us on our way to stardom.

Agna strongly questioned the existence of a place where satisfaction and peace comes natural to everyone. She argued persistently with Ela who had some faith that Liberty indeed existed.

Most people who got to Liberty Dancehouse doubted the existence of a place where they can find motivation and joy. Thus, when they got to the Dancehouse, by one means or the other, they confirmed that there indeed exist a reality that is bigger and better than they had imagined.

Often, what we call "reality" is but one aspect of the Big Picture. While we may have been led to believe that our version of reality is the only one or the best one, there may be other versions of reality that can help us if we are open to learn from them. The joy of true learning lies in discovering ever-new and more rewarding aspects of the Big Picture and expanding our understanding of how big reality truly is!

I think it is ignorance that makes us assume that our experiences and beliefs are the only ones that exist. Usually, we are unaware of the bigger or at least other realities that exist outside of our own. Thus we tend to believe that our own reality is ubiquitous.

There exists many different cultures and races around the world. It is thus ethnocentric to believe that the rules, values, and beliefs of one's culture are the only ones that are valid. It is a delimiting mentality.

Every person around us has different values and theirs are not necessarily better or worse than ours. The key question is not whether the values are right or wrong, but whether they empower or disempower us. A belief system is basically built up from thoughts and such thoughts may be based on some cultural experiences, social lessons, environmental knowledge, scientific discovery or personal conviction. It is very important to remain open to new ways of seeing things. They say a new discovery is not seeing new landscapes but having new eyes. Everyone needs a constant renewal of the mind.

When in conversation with others who seem to disagree with our position about a thing, we must not be quick to disprove their positions. Most times, different people are speaking from different perspectives, experiences or knowledge base which justify and validate their positions. Their put downs could be as valid as ours.

The difference is in the context and their perspective of the topic being discussed. It is easy to strongly challenge the position of others on a topic, especially when it negates our own value systems. However, it is important to respect *where they are coming from.*

As a personal example. I usually feel uneasy when people try to justify gays and gay marriages and that's because of my cultural, religious and personal convictions. I will naturally want to impose my position on others in a bid to disprove their opinions.

However, I should understand that other opinions and perspectives indeed exist like: biological explanations and psychological positions which are possibly worth listening to. I do not have to agree with these other opinions as they deeply violate my beliefs, but it is wisdom to agree that there are in fact other perspectives that are different from mine. In these cases, we agree to differ on the point of discussion.

And this is fine.

When we open ourselves to embrace and learn from other realities, we give ourselves the opportunity to explore our endless possibilities.

Upgrade your Relationships

"Everyone needs a translator. A friend who hears what you cannot hear"

There is a famous monkey experiment I heard the other day. A group of scientists placed bananas on the top of a ladder in a cage. Then they placed four monkeys in the cage. Every time a monkey climbed the ladder to reach the banana, the scientists soaked the rest of the monkeys with cold water. When a monkey subsequently tries to climb the ladder, the others would pull it down and beat it up.

After a while, no monkey dared to climb the ladder, no matter how tempted they got. The scientists then decided to replace one of the monkeys. The new monkey immediately tried to climb the ladder to the banana. As expected, the others pulled it down and beat it up.

After several beatings, the new monkey learned never to go up the ladder, even though there was no evident reason not to, asides the beatings. The second monkey was substituted and the same occurred. The first monkey this time, participated in the beating of the second monkey. The third and fourth monkeys were replaced and the same was repeated.

What was left then was a group of four monkeys that – without ever having received a cold shower – continued to beat up any monkey that attempted to climb the ladder. They had no idea why they did this. They just knew it was the way it was done. They simply did things that they saw others do.

"We must constantly ask ourselves these questions: Who am I around? What are they doing to me? What have they got me reading? What have they got me saying? Where do they have me going? What do they have me thinking? And most important: What do they have me becoming? Then ask yourself the big question: Is that okay? Your life does not get better by chance, it gets better by change." – Jim Rohn.

"You are where you are today because you have chosen to be there." - Harry Brown.

We are essentially products of our choices and decisions. A crucial part of such decisions is of the people we spend our time and life with. Our lives have been hugely affected by the kinds of people we have allowed in our lives till now. It is thus important to constantly do a deliberate check of the values and influences we receive from people around us, else, like our dear monkeys, we may live in error and think of it as the norm.

The impression from Louis was very profound: *"Everyone needs a translator, a friend who hears what you cannot hear."* Every relationship in our lives should complement our weaknesses, not expose them. Every relationship that does not add any significant value to us is unhealthy. We either get better or get worse by the relationships we keep, there are no middle grounds.

Thus it is important to create a positive atmosphere around ourselves. This forces us to live a consistent, ever increasing quality of life. We must consciously maintain an environment where growth is a must! In effect, we will ensure that only valuable relationships are accommodated in our lives and all demeaning relationships will naturally fade away.

In our aim to create a growth-oriented atmosphere around us, we must aim for relationships where:

- we are growing
- we are challenged to do greater things
- others are growing
- others complement and encourage us
- failure is not feared
- change is embraced

Turn Deaf

"If the music is boring, change it or turn deaf!"

Everyone thinks of light bulbs when they hear the name - Thomas Alva Edison. He is clearly the greatest inventive genius in the world, with 1093 American patented inventions to his name - a record number for one person that still stands. His inventions include the phonograph - one of the earliest motion picture projectors, and the incandescent light bulb, among several others. All these made Edison a hero!

Like many other heroes, his story was not without a clog. Around the age of 12, Edison realized that his hearing was deteriorating, and this grew worse later in his life. He became hard of hearing, almost deaf; as were his father, and son, Charles. His deafness has been attributed to various things: a childhood illness, ear infections that went untreated, genetics, accidents, etc.

There he was, a twelve-year-old Edison largely self-taught. Teachers thought Edison was slow - one called him stupid - so he was homeschooled by his mother and read constantly. He shunned every disbelief and malign influences of his teacher's comments. He was cooped up with his mother every day, reading and learning.

And see how he turned out.

Reporters often asked him: "Mr. Edison why, if you are near deaf, have you not invented a hearing aid?"

"I'm working on one - for others." He would reply. "As for me, I find there are distinct advantages to being deaf. For one, it forces me to read, and reading beats the babble of ordinary conversation. For another, it helps me concentrate on my work and spend less time answering foolish questions from individuals such as yourself. Deafness allowed me to work with less distraction and to sleep deeply, undisturbed by outside sounds."

Edison saw his deafness as an asset! "To invent, you need a

good imagination, a pile of junk *and some deafness*." He often said.

How is that for a lesson? To invent, you need … some deafness. Period!

It is the fear instilled by other people's opinions that mostly limit us. We are often distracted and discouraged by the noises of other people's experiences. Many times, negative external influences are the major reasons we do not take actions for what we believe in. People tend to set limits for our successes based on their own limits. And usually, we personalized the failures of others and assume we will fail in the same.

However, the fact that others failed in a thing, does not mean we will fail in the same. Other people's realities do not define your reality. Life races are personalized, you do not compete against others but yourself. Your track is personal and unique.

One major secret to being creative and successful in anything we do is the ability to shun all negative external influences and doubts about our ingenuity. Limiting opinions of others about us should not discourage us from reaching for our absolute best.

Steve Jobs said: "Your time is limited, so don't waste it living someone else's life. Don't be trapped by dogma – which is living with the results of other people's thinking. Don't let the noise of other's opinions drown out your own inner voice. And most important, have the courage to follow your heart and intuition. They somehow already know what you truly want to become. Everything else is secondary."

It is delimiting to live based on other people's expectations of us. "I'm not in this world to live up to your expectations and you're not in this world to live up to mine." - Bruce Lee.

It takes courage to shun all discouragements in a bid to stay focused on our truest dreams. In order to reach our dreams, we must seek strength to make clear decisions and to stand by them. We mostly make wrong decisions when we are in a wrong emotional state.

Emotions such as weakness, tiredness, loneliness, hunger, anger etc. weaken our decision making. These feelings naturally increase our chances of making wrong decisions and push us to consider short-sighted solutions. When we feel negative, we feel the need to satisfy our immediate needs and usually decide based on this need.

Essentially, people who give advices talk based on their care and interest to make us feel good and meet our immediate needs. So the intention of the advisor is in fact well-meaning and should be appreciated. The problem however is in the advice itself. Does it ultimately move us towards our goal or does it just solve an immediate problem?

The popular Bible story of Esau and Jacob gives a perfect example. Profane Esau got home hungry and asked his younger brother, Jacob for soup. Jacob decided to strike a deal with his brother. He would have his brother trade his position as firstborn for a small plate of food. Esau was not thinking right when he agreed to the deal. Once Jacob became the firstborn, all the rights and blessings accruing to the firstborn came on him – and those were priceless.

It is important to delay making important decisions when we feel negative emotions. In the same manner, it is important to stay careful in making promises when we feel ecstatically happy; there is a high chance of making high-sounding promises that we are unable to fulfill.

So, if the music is boring, change it or turn deaf.

References

Chapter One:
Kehinde Fawumi (2009). "Tomorrow's Realities Today"

Chapter Two:
"Success can be measured by the magnitude of the obstacles overcome to achieve it" – Quote by Booker T. Washington
Steve Jobs'commencement speech at Stanford University (2005): "How to live before you die"
Kehinde Fawumi (2009). "Tomorrow's Realities Today"

Chapter Three:
Dr. Spencer Johnson (1998). "Who moved my Cheese"
Giles Andreae (2008). "Giraffes Can't Dance"

Chapter Four:
"To dance is to be out of yourself. Larger, more beautiful, more powerful." – Quote by Agnes de Mille
Giles Andreae (2008). "Giraffes Can't Dance"

Chapter Five:
Steve Jobs'commencement speech at Stanford University (2005): "How to live before you die"
Dr Myles Munroe (2011). "Understanding Your Place in God's Kingdom: Your Original Purpose for Existence."
Kehinde Fawumi (2009). "Tomorrow's Realities Today"
James Dobson (1993). "When God Doesn't Make Sense"
Sam Adeyemi (2015). "Your Mind Is Your Most Important Asset"
Tony Robbins (1992), "Awaken the Giant Within"
Joyce Bedi (2004). " Thomas Edison's Inventive Life"
C. L. Kelly (2009) "Echo. A silent plea to be heard, a desperate cry to be found"